I Sure Do! Grandparents

Dr. Ted Steliotes

To my mom, Ann Steliotes, who is **so** loved by my son, Leonidas and me. He loves playing "stinky feet" with her.

To my grandparents, James and Demetra Steliotes and James and Anna Dattilo.

About the Author

Dr. Ted Steliotes is an award-winning dentist in Pennsylvania. He is a graduate of the University of Dayton, where he received his BS in biology and psychology. He earned his dental degree at the University of Pittsburgh School Of Dental Medicine and finished his residency at UCLA in California. Dr. Steliotes is the official dentist for the contestants of the Miss and Teen USA Pageants. Dr. Steliotes has always used his visionary gifts to write children's books.

Who likes to eat ice cream with Grandad in a bowl bigger than your hands?

I Sure Do!

Who likes to play the stinky feet game with Grandma? Pee-u!

I Sure Do!

Who likes to eat animal shaped pancakes with lots of syrup that Grandma made?

I Sure Do!

Who likes making cookies, cakes and pretzels dripped in chocolate with Grandma?

I Sure Do!

Who likes having Grandma pack a picnic lunch for you and Grandad to eat while fishing at a nearby pond?

I Sure Do!

Who likes dressing up in Grandma and Grandad's old clothes?

I Sure Do!

Who likes to have Grandma or Grandad read your favorite book to you?

I Sure Do!

Who likes to play board games with Grandad and scream "I Won, I Won!" when you win?

I Sure Do!

Who likes to paint a "masterpiece" to hang on Grandma and Grandad's refrigerator?

I Sure Do!

Who likes to go shopping for a new toy with Grandma and Grandad?

I Sure Do!

Who likes to ride horsey on
Grandad's back?
"Ride-m-cowboy"!!

I Sure Do!

Who likes to help Grandma roll meatballs for spaghetti dinner?

I Sure Do!

Who likes to look at old pictures of your parents when they were your age? Grandparents love to tell stories from the "old days".

I Sure Do!

Who likes to snuggle on the couch with Grandad eating popcorn and watching movies?

I Sure Do!

Who loves their grandparents just because they are **so awesome**?

I Sure Do!!!!

Other books by Dr. Ted Steliotes

The Sleepy Time Train

Good Morning, Good Morning, Good Morning to you!

How Did You Get So Cute?

I Sure Do! Bedtime

I Sure Do! Christmas

A portion of the proceeds from this book will be donated to:

THE SMILE TRAIN

Smile Train provides free cleft palate repair surgeries to those in need while helping to train local doctors. This makes it possible for a child born with a cleft palate to eat, breathe, speak properly and smile.

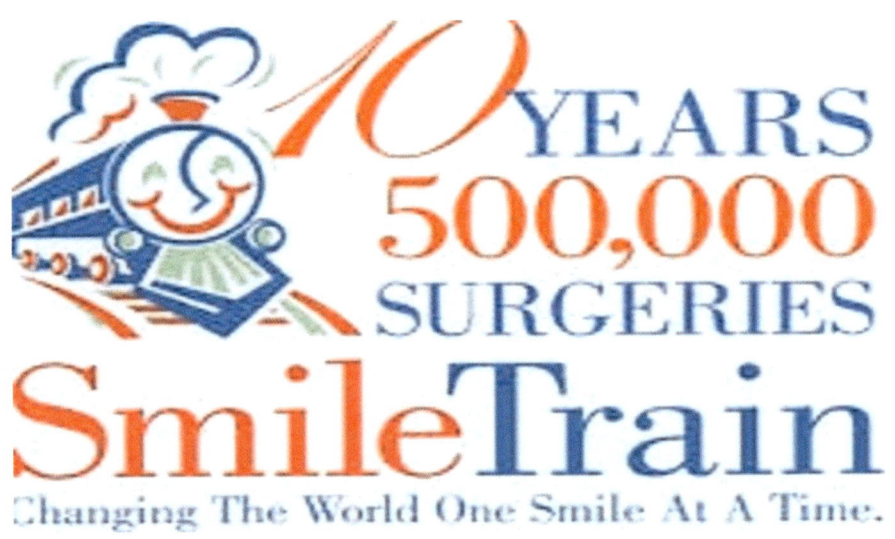

Made in the USA
Coppell, TX
23 September 2021